"THE UNELECTED PRESIDENT"

"Operation Just Cause"

My suggestion for the
United States Invasion of Panama

By

Harvey Carroll, Jr.

Richmond man says he helped organize Panama invasion, war

By Chad Carlton
Herald-Leader staff writer

If what Harvey Carroll Jr. says is to be believed, he is the most influential international political figure in Kentucky.

Among his claims:

● Named and planned "Operation Just Cause," the U.S. military strike that deposed Panamanian dictator Manuel Noriega.

"I told my CIA contact, 'Why don't we go in with low-intensity action to bring him in,'" Carroll said.

● Helped organize the coalition support for "Operation Desert Storm," the war against Iraq.

"I wasn't a Schwarzkopf out there in the desert," he said. "But I do think my suggestions did bring about a quick end to the war."

Harvey Carroll Jr.

Age: 27

Residence: Richmond

This is my third book; however, I recently published a near 30 page Poem on "Desert Storm," after that my Mini-Autobiography "THE UNELECTED PRSIDENT), and then SCREWED, which is about the Lewinsky sex scandal and my involvement in Clinton's "Little White House Lie."

I intend to publish a series of Books under the trademark
"THE UNELECTED PRESIDENT"
ISBN-13:
978-1530001460

ISBN-10:
1530001463

DEDICATION

My book is dedicated to those working with drug related Political Policy Making at the community, local, state, national and international levels.

Yet, it is mainly for those within the Law Enforcement Community that are on the front lines of the vast drug related crime problems. I understand your difficulties...

It's also dedicated to the millions of not only Americas, but people from around the World that face drug addictions and/or have family and/or friends that deal with addictions. It's tough, I've seen and dealt with it...

To all, stay the course and do what you can to help... Try to encourage those with problems that they should have a long-term view on life and begin to set goals that reflect the life that they want to have...............

"Operation Just Cause"

CONTENTS

Acknowledgments   Pg-i

1   GENERAL MANUEL A. NORIEGA   Pg-1
HIS PATH TO BECOMING A
DRUG INDICTED DICTATOR

2   BIBLE STUDY TO BLOOD BATH   Pg-7

3   OPOSING VIEWS   Pg-18
"THE PANAMA DECEPTION"

4   SNEP'S ARTICLE IN PLAYBOY   Pg-26

5   EVEN MORE I DIDN'T KNOW-   Pg-38
IRAN CONTRA AFFAIR;
DRUGS, GUNS AND JIHAD

6   ATTENTION CONSTRUCTIVE   Pg-45
POLICY MAKERS

7   BUILD A WALL OR BUILD   Pg-50
SOCIETY

ABOUT THE AUTHOR   Pg-56

ACKNOWLEDGMENTS

We as Policy Makers must try harder not to make mistakes. We must focus on the 3D's—Democracy, Diplomacy and Development... Especially when it affects so many dear and precious lives..

I strongly feel that all communities, and cities throughout the World need to focus on "Comprehensive Planning" to create growth and development, and more Global focus on PESTEL politics as opposed to pistol politics...

1
GENERAL MANUEL A. NORIEGA HIS PATH TO BECOMING A DRUG INDICTED DICTATOR

Manuel A. Noriega was born on February 11, 1934 in Panama City, Panama. At the age of 5 he was given up for adoption to a schoolteacher.

It was reported that Noriega when growing up he wanted to be a Doctor but was not fortunate enough to have the money to pay for college. Instead he attended a military academy for college. Noriega later became the head of The National Guard of Panama in 1983.

In 1989 he seized control of Panama and also declared war on the United States. This was a big mistake...

Panama was not only the primary shipping route, but also a vital strategic national security point of interest for the United States. The U.S. had military bases and vast covert establishments within and near Panama.

We should also add that it was American money that was used for the building and developing the Canal. The U. S. has had to deal with a lot of uprisings and flair ups that American suppressed. To list of few of the more noted flare ups: [1]

o In 1913 the U. S. began a strong military buildup in the Canal Zone, which wasn't popular with the locals.

o Various others flair ups by 1960.

o 1964 when 21 people were killed and hundreds wounded in a violent protest to force the U. S. allow the Panamanian to fly their Flag.

---

[1] For an interesting perspective on the history of Panama leading up to the Invasion, see: "Confessions of an Economic Hit Man", by John Perkins (Published by Plume, a member of Penguin Group (USA), Inc.), Pg. 67.

o In 1968 Omar Torrijos took the country by coup, and initiated some popular social reforms. To the best of my knowledge the C.I.A. supported Torrijos's take over.

o In 1978 Torrijos established relations with U. S. President Jimmy Carter, which signed a treaty that would turn the Canal back over to the Panamanian people in the year 2,000.

Noriega became the head of the Panamanian National Guard. I was graduating high school, and on my way to the U.S. Army Military Police in 1983.

I'm not sharing my Military Police Investigator Appraisal Report from a special IRR Assignment at Fort Bliss, TX in 1988, but I can tell you it was good and welcoming back into the Army and/or Military Police Investigations if I choose to return.

Yet, I had no intentions to return to the Army or Military Police. I had larger ambitions back in Kentucky Politics. Yet, I can clearly point out that National and International Politics was on my mind. I had seen a fellow MPI Agents brains laying on his car related to Drug Investigations...

NOTE: This traumatic event left me very conservative on the "War on Drugs."

The United States had a number of reasons to invade Panama. The main reason was to bring Noriega to trial in the United States for drug trafficking charges. I as well as the Unites States thought Noriega had become a serious threat to the United States.

The United States also had to protect our 35,000 Americans in Panama. Noriega was responsible for the shotting and death of a U.S. marine in December 1989 after he had declared a state of war with the United States.

It was reasonable for the U.S. to want to bring democracy back to Panama. In about ten years the U.S. would have to turn the Panama Canal to the Panamanians. It was in the U.S. best interest to keep control of the Panama Canal if Panama had a radical Anti-U.S. leader...

His own people wanted to take him out of power also. Noriega was not a good leader for his country. Noriega built a "Strongman Military" that put him in a position to pick and choose who he wanted to lead Panama.

There were many tales of Noriega putting people in prison and/or killing them for voicing their public criticisms...

He had his people against him, the opposition against him, much of the military, and the United States...

The odds had become stacked against the Drug Indicted Dictator abusing his people, Americans and his flea on the America Flag declaration of War against the United States...

2
BIBLE STUDY TO BLOOD BATH

I was in New York working. I was there working to provide security along with many other ex-military types during the New York Daily News labor dispute. A very tough and violent strike that I and friends tried to keep from getting out of hand...

While out to eat for the evening I came across a Bible chat... At this time I was not a very religious man. I had been out to eat at a place called "Victoria Station" a cool place with connecting Train Cabooses turned into a restaurant near Yonkers, New York.

At Victoria's Station, near Yonkers, New York I met a couple really nice ladies. I chatted with a bit about the Bible and was invited to a bible study. I agree and one of their friends came over as agreed and took me to the host home. After the bible study I met the host.

That discussion changed me and the World many times...

Seriously, talk about "Divine Intervention" or just pure fate. Three months before the December 1989 invasion of Panama just happened to watch General Manuel Noriega pounding a sword on a podium. He was in total rage and defiance against the United States.

The host in private conversations claimed to be a former Latin American C.I.A. Intelligence Agent. He presented me with a card and told me that he was currently working as an Intelligence Analyst for the Drug Enforcement Agency.

NOTE:COPY OF CARD ON FILE WITH MY OPM FEDERAL BACKGROUND INVESTIGATION THAT I PASSED.....

Being a former Military Policeman, I had a bit of a conservative view on drugs. I felt that hard-core drugs had to be stopped before they reached the U.S. therefore, I stated:

I simply said...

- If you guys, the D.E.A. has enough evidence on Noriega, why doesn't the U. S. simply go in with low-intensity conflict. Apprehend Noriega and bring him back to the U.S. on drug charges and money laundering charges; similar to the way an organized crime leader "Bunt Gross" got busted in my hometown of Irvine, KY".

- To save lives and deter a lot of shots from being fired. The U.S. could go in with a strong perception of power, with large convoys of helicopter gun ships.

- Name it something like "Operation Just Cause", because it is a just cause to keep hard core drugs from entering the U.S...

The Intelligence Agent looked at me and said "hummm interesting"...

Three months later, the Panamanian invasion better known as "Operation Just Cause" began on December 19th, 1989. The midnight raid dropped about 29,000 American Troops into Panama supported by swarms of helicopters.

I watched my suggestions for "Operation Just Cause" on TV. Yet, there was considerable extra overkill added... I was quite shocked to see such intensity...

The U.S. Southern Command under the leadership of General Maxwell R. Thurman decided to drop 29,000 troops into Panama. It was far from the low intensity conflict, that I had suggested... https://en.wikipedia.org/wiki/Maxwel l_R._Thurman

For the next few days I stayed glued to the TV to see if I could get involved and/or assist in any way. When I saw issues.

https://en.wikipedia.org/wiki/United_States_invasion_of_Panama

Verbatim Text from the link of the forces that went into Panama:

"The US Army, Air Force, Navy, and Marines participated in Operation Just Cause. Ground forces consisted of :

- combat elements of the XVIII Airborne Corps,
- the 82nd Airborne Division,
- the 7th Infantry Division (Light),
- the 7th Special Force Group (Airborne),
- the 75th Ranger Regiment,
- a Joint Special Operations Task Force,
- elements of the 5th Infantry Division

- 1st Battalion, 61st U.S. Infantry and
- 4th Battalion, 6th United States Infantry (replacing 1/61st in September 1989)),
- 1138th Military Police Company of the Missouri Army National Guard,
- 988 Military Police Company out of Ft. Benning, GA
- 193rd Infantry Brigade,
  - 5th Battalion, 87th Infantry
  - 1st Battalion, 508th Infantry,
  - Battery D, 320th Field Artillery
- 59th Engineer Company,
- Marine Security Forces Battalion Panama,
- Kilo company of 3rd Battalion, 6th Marine Regiment,
- Marine Fleet Antiterrorism Security Teams,
- 2nd Light Armored Reconnaissance Battalion,

- 2nd Marine Logistics Group 39th Combat Engineer Btn. Charlie Co."

I also began to make a few suggestions as "if" I were running the operation. I made the following suggestions which ended up happening. The first was to find Noriega...

- Mainly President Bush address the American public call General Manuel Noriega a Narco-Terrorist and a Drug related, indicted, dictator.

I watched a variety of assertive action take place in the attempt to extradite Manual Noriega.[2]

  o Bush also stated several times that he wanted to see him out of there (Panama).

---

[2] Most all national news stations during "Operation Just Cause" the Panama Invasion.

- I suggested that Bush place a million dollar reward for information that led to the apprehension of Noriega with a Washington, DC, number (202) 633-1000.

- In addition, I suggested that General Noriega to be pointed out by the President as "running the country under a form of Mafiaism instead of Democracy".

Overall the media pools were controlled perfectly by the military and pretty much that of which was supposed to make the news made it.

By watching the news like millions of other Americans I was proud of the Panama Invasion and what the U. S. had accomplished there. However, I begin to look at the deeper concerns between god and evil, ethics and what makes up a civil society. I pondered policy and the complexities and sometimes two-face approaches to policy making...

The Panama Invasion "Operation Just Cause" resulted in the final Assault on La Comandancia, Panama City, Panama, December 1989.

"Operation Just Cause" was one of the shortest armed conflicts in American military history; it was also one of the largest low intensity conflicts that were an overkill operation compared to my "helicopter gunship" suggestions...

"Operation Just Cause" was one of the most sophisticated joint contingency operations of its time led by the elite 82nd Airborne Division along with 29,000 America troops. I was sadden to see them dropped into Panama to apprehend the drug indicted Dictator General Manuel Noriega. It was quite a bit different from my suggestions...

This was a TV War. Americans displayed the invasion on television and rallied around it; thereby, invoking nationalism. Granted some TV news casters became part of the story. These news producers were captured and held as hostages. They were threatened with ak-47 by Panamanians who were loyal to Noriega. TV loved the coverage...

The overkill operation got American killed, and some 5,000 Panamanians according to a documentary called "The Panama Deception"...

The operation also got a Fraternity Pledge Brother's brother from my undergraduate college EKU killed.

I have also met Panamanians that lost family, and mothers who lost sons... It is always a sad and uncomfortable discussion to realize that you know that you made a suggestion that cost someone his or her loved ones life...

Drugs, is a war within our-selves to take them; even when you're in prolonged pain...

Years later I had major surgery, and have been in serious pain. I still tried to focus on avoiding drugs and focused on embracing the pain more than drugs...

War on Drugs is a war within ourselves, we should choose Education and Accomplishment as the Drug of Choice...

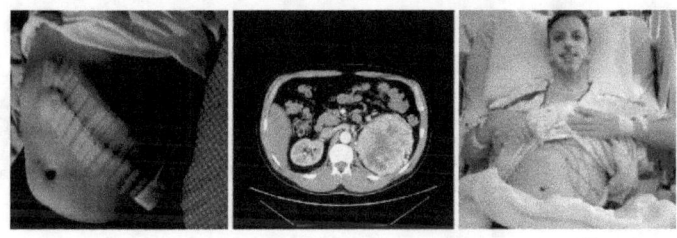

"Avoiding drug addiction is the key, one should try to be more productive and focus on Education, and making Education the "Drug of Choice"... .
~Harvey Carroll, Jr.

Drug Abuse kills--We have seen it with many Celebrities such as Whitney Houston; hence "A war on drugs -vs- a war within ourselves to take drugs"...

3
OPOSING VIEWS
"THE PANAMA DECEPTION"

However, I later conducted research and watched a film called the "The Panama Deception" narrated by Elisabeth Montgomery "Bewitched." I then became somewhat disturbed and distressed about the invasion.

The film presented a totally different perception than the press had portrayed it. According to the film, thousands of people lost their lives and nearly twenty thousand Panamanian homes were systematically burnt and destroyed by the U. S. Military.

This in my opinion was totally uncalled for and could have been avoided. I feel that the Ground Commander in charge of the U. S. Southern Command in Panama should have taken full responsibility for the excessive use of force.

These were not my suggestions of going in with large convoys of helicopter gunships as a show of force to avoid shots from being fired. Yet, the Devil was in the details and the U.S. Southern Command ended up using extreme excessive use of force which cost many lives during the Panama Invasion.

To summarize the film, recorded history of U. S. /Panama relations revealed that since the 1800's the U.S. has refused to acknowledge Panama's independence.

Covert activities have been part of the U. S. policy since about 1903, which enabled Panama to break free of Columbia rule. The French undertook a effort that the ended in financial disaster. President Theodore Roosevelt backed the French and sent warships to the region killing war lords and declared Panama an independent nation[3]

The U. S. then secured rights from French investors to obtain sovereign control in perpetuity. The ten-mile wide tract of land called The Canal Zone was obviously essential to the United States international trade and commerce and greatly enhanced Panama's economic future, as well as opening up the entire Latin American region.

From watching the news over the past few decades it is pretty obvious that the Reagan and Bush administration opposed most policies that President Carter was involved in. They undermined his dealings in Iran with the "Iran Contra Scandal" as well as running covert operations into Latin America on that violated Congressional Mandates.

---

[3] For an interesting perspective on the history of Panama leading up to the Invasion, see: "Confessions of an Economic Hit Man", by John Perkins (Published by Plume, a member of Penguin Group (USA), Inc.), Pg. 67.

Many think that after the Reagan Administration won the Presidency in 1980 and the Panamanian dictator Omar Torrijos mysteriously dying in a plane crash was more than a coincidence. Sergeant Chuchu, alias Jose De Jesus Martinez[4] has been on record suspecting that the plane was blown up by C.I.A.. Others as have I saw speculative associations between the C.I.A. and Noriega.

This led me to consider the thought that perhaps since the plane was downed over Panama, that the C.I.A. used then friendly General Manual Noriega to do the dirty work and blow it out of the sky. Then again, it could just be plain green on behalf of Noriega or any of the many drug thugs that wanted to rise in power by destroying

---

[4] For an interesting perspective and allegation that the C.I.A. blew up Omar Torrijos plane strait from his security guard, see: "Confessions of an Economic Hit Man", by John Perkins (Published by Plume, a member of Penguin Group (USA), Inc.), Pg. 67.

the existing President of Panama.

The C.I.A. as well as a lot of business entities (which we will discuss later) that have economic interest in Latin America have been involved in Paramilitary Training in the "School of The Americas" managed by the U.S. Southern Command. General Torrijos and Carter planned on shutting it down according to John Perkins with his verbatim statements.[5]

"Declassified documents confirm that Noriega had been a primary C.I.A. contact since the 1960's. In 1976 during the Ford administration Bush was appointed the Director of The Central Intelligence Agency. Director Bush increased Noriega's covert paycheck to

---

[5] For an interesting perspective on the closing of The School of The Americas and the U.S. Southern Command's tropical warfare center., see: "Confessions of an Economic Hit Man", by John Perkins (Published by Plume, a member of Penguin Group (USA), Inc.), Pg. 187.

over $100,000 a year.

Bush later as Vice President of the United States was in charge of the nation's Anti-Drug campaign. Noriega was responsible for many D.E.A (Drug Enforcement Administration part of the U. S. Dept. of Justice) international drug and money laundering arrest by supplying intelligence reports to the D.E.A..

"By 1983 Noriega had become a Latin American strong man dealing with his powerful covert connections. He was a major player in the Iran-Contra Scandal by assisting Col. Oliver North who was running guns into Northern Costa-Rico; where Noriega arranged the pickup and delivery of the weapons to the Sandinistas, which were sold as the "Freedom Fighters" by President Reagan." [6]

---

[6] "The Panama Deception", Film Verbatim Summary, narrated by Elizabeth Montgomery. (Further

The impact for the American society was that of more drugs and guns on the streets. This of course threatened communities, law enforcement and created chaos through the rise of gangs.

The big loss was far less focus on education and civil society? There are still drugs coming to the United States from South American and Mexico.

Many felt that the Unites States had broken international laws and its own government police by invading Panama. I felt that it was justified to finally have a real "War on Drugs."

Others like myself, thought it to be a "Just Cause" and with Noriega out of power there should be a real slow down of drug flow from South American to the United States.

Sadly, my "War on Drugs" via

---

information unknown)

"Operation Just Cause" the United States Invasion of Panama turned out to be counterproductive. The Blunders of "Son" George W. Bush policies led to economic problems that increased drug problems throughout America.

Welfare rose from 17 to 45 million, nearly 80 million Americas ended up in poverty. Trade Imbalance tripped to nearly 1 Trillion a Year. Housing values dropped nearly 40 percent nationally, millions of Americans lost the American Dream along with their homes, cars, and even families... Many turned to drugs...

4
SNEP'S ARTICLE IN PLAYBOY

Weirdly, I found an old copy of Playboy on my dad's farm in a box full of old newspapers and magazines used to start fires. Once past the Centerfold, I found the cool article written by Snep that discussed Panama. It also mentioned Perot that I would later meet and vies as a political mentor in Presidential Politics...

To go one step further, I read an article "The Company He keeps" in "Play Boy" written by Frank Snepp who covered the Iran-contra scandal for ABC News. He writes about how Ross Perot's name had popped up in the strangest places, such as in Oliver North's notebooks.

According to Snepp; Perot first met North in the early Seventies, and had actually talked North out of quitting the Marine Corps. This chance meeting later lead both men into the thickets of covert action.

After Ronald Reagan was elected President, Perot began working closely with the White House and began to work with North. Perot was noted as working with a couple key White House groups.

- o The Intelligence Support Activity and,
- o President's Foreign Intelligence Advisory Board.

Snepp mentioned that Perot also boasted about how he hired paramilitary teams to exchange money for hostages. This ended up being a political night mare for President Carter holding the hostages until Regan entered the White House.

According to Snepp, verbatim statement; [7]

---

[7] "The Company He keeps" in "Play Boy" written by

"in May 1985, at North's request, Perot offered $200,000 to help ransom CIA station chief William Buckley, seized in Lebanon a year earlier. Perot pledged another several million dollars to pay off the kidnappers through a drug dealer in Beirut. As it happened, the down payment disappeared into an unidentified pocket and Buckley died in captivity".

As I spent many of my college days glued to the Iran-contra scandal hearings on TV the names of billionaire Perot, President, Reagan and Bush and Col Oliver North[8] and others were being investigated and named in a variety of lawsuits.

In addition, to a variety of allegations and later indictments of drug traffickers that participated in the

---

Frank Snepp, who covered the Iran-contra scandal for ABC News. (Further Information Unknown)

[8] TIME magazine photo of Oliver North.

contra-support effort as well as U.S. Intelligence and D.E.A agents were dragged into closed session hearings and some were also indicted.

Snepp wrote that Perot stated, "Guys got into the habit of using drugs to raise money to finance anti-communist operations, and they can't break themselves of the habit."[9] The illegal Iran-Contra scandal revealed the vast details of the worldwide drug-and-weapons network and cover-up via his verbatim text;

---

[9] "The Company He keeps" in "Play Boy" written by Frank Snepp, who covered the Iran-contra scandal for ABC News. (Further Information Unknown)

"In the mid 1980's it was becoming clearer that Noriega was not under total control of the U. S.. At the 1984 Condodora Peace talks Noriega called for the U. S. to stay out of Latin American policies. This created some problems with the future of Noriega.

In 1986 the Iran-Contra Scandal exploded and Noriega became visible. In order to save face with the U. S. and justify his C.I.A. payroll there were over 100 D.E.A drug related arrest and millions of dollars in assets frozen due to Noriega being a U. S. informant code-named "Operation Pieces".

"Later the U. S. accused Noriega himself of murder and corruption, which sparked off a wave of oppression, which was led to President Reagan calling for Noriega to step down as the leader of Panama. In addition, there were a variety of sanctions places on Panama; however, General Noriega seamed to avoid the influence that sanctions are designed to do because he was participating/profiting from the black market drug trade."[10]

Then in Feb. 1988 two U. S. Federal Grand Juries indicted Noriega on money laundering and Racketeering charges. He was the first foreign head of state ever to be indicted by the American Government. The rest is history, my history as you read at the beginning...

There are a couple of things come to my mind after reflecting back on the Invasion. First, my sincere condolences go out to the thousands of Panamanians who lost their lives, and/or their homes. I truly think that the US Southern Command used excessive forces.

---

[10] Verbatim Text from "The Company He keeps" in "Play Boy" written by Frank Snepp who covered the Iran-contra scandal for ABC News. (Further Information Unknown)

I wasn't on the ground and in a military operation you have to allow desecration and a certain amount of faith that they made the right decisions at the time to achieve the mission. I still feel that the end was justified and the perception of the heightened drug war saved exponentially the amount of lives that were sacrifices.

Then there are the people that I've met that were affected personally. I think of the huge Marine that I met while I was out drinking beer and shooting pool at a college hang out in Richmond, KY. He said he had read something about me in the paper and my involvement in the Panama Invasion. So, I told him that was me and that I had made the suggestion.

He said he laid in a the Walter Reed Hospital bed ridden for about six months and he hoped to meet the idiot that planed the invasion so he could get the chance to kick their ass. I told him he got his chance to go ahead and get it over with. Then he said that he finely concluded that it was a worthwhile operation and even though the U. S. utilized excessive force it should save hundreds of thousands of lives in the future.

I respected and agreed with his opinion, because, I always felt that the end would justify the means, because there truly are way too many lives destroyed by drugs each year. Plus, bar brawls is never a good thing. Win or lose you still end up a bit sore the next day. I might add that I've never lost a bar brawl, but it isn't something that I go looking for either.

So, we had another beer and shot a game of pool. He told me about spending six months in Walter Reed Hospital near Washington, D.C. after being shot in the arm in Panama. He said the bullet hit him so hard that it twisted his entire body and broke both ankles.

Hence the six months contemplating the ass kicking. Lucky for me he was doing fine now.

Second, a pledge brother of a college fraternity comes to mind. His biological brother was killed during the assault in Panama. I had deep empathy for him, and I know that there is no way that I can ever understand his loss or replace his brother. I understood his loss much deeper when I lost my brother in a car accident in January 2001. Yet, with the Fraternity he found other brothers that will be with him all throughout his life.

Third, a political acquaintance I met on the Internet whom had lost her son. We discussed via several emails the concept of the Panama Invasion and how her son would have been proud to participate in such a noble venture. I of course offered my sincere condolences for her loss.

Fourth, a Co-worker Carlos Roberts, who is now living in Florida, provided me with some of the devastation photos of the Panama Invasion.[11]

I guess by now you can see a pattern of people's lives that I affected in some way; mainly with death, but let's try to put it in real perspective. Are we going to allow drug thugs to control our streets, our schools and our economy? Or are we going to take action and use our military, police, and intelligence organization and American educational institutions to take them back and have a constructive influence on our future.

The youth will be responsible for taking care of our baby-boomers one million dollar each estimated retirement responsibilities. Unless we shift to socialized medicine they will have one

---

[11] Panama Invasion damage photos by Carlos Robert a friend who once worked with Interpol.

heavy burden to support us. They can't do it if they are uneducated and unemployable due to drugs. I will address this issue more in following chapters...

NOTE: (My association with the Agent was confirmed by a Federal Background Investigation conducted on me in 1994. For obvious reason I will never reveal the agents name.

Snep stated that in their business "if" he was one of theirs, which he wasn't; then he isn't going to go out of his way to give me much credit."

The CIA agent that I talked with told me that he had been used a bit in the past also. He reminded me of the "The old dog eats dog philosophy" and people are going to use others for their benefit if they can. The agent benefited a great deal from our discussions. Not that that is a bad thing.

I wish him the best of luck in his

career and I think that this country owes him a debt of gratitude for having the ability to disseminate and pass on quality advice. In fact, I think he is doing OK, I did know that he got a cushy job in Washington, D.C. where I kept in contact for a while).

The discussion ended with the C.I.A. Official stating that "The Central Intelligence Agency doesn't give out letters of recommendation." With this in mind it was pretty tough as you might imagine substantiating some of my claims of Presidential Level Involvement and/or dealing with National and International Affairs.

I do what I can with the resources that I have… If you read my books, you will see that I have done quite well with little to no resources...

5
EVEN MORE I DIDN'T KNOW-
IRAN CONTRA AFFAIR;
DRUGS, GUNS AND JIHAD

Bad Policy Making "Iran Contra Affair" and "Drugs, Guns and Jihad"

The Iran Contra Affair under the Direction of U.S. President Ronald Reagan, Vice President Bush, CIA William Casey and Col. Oliver North built a covert coalition between the Mujahedeen/Radial Islamist of the Muslim Brotherhood, the Saudi Royal Family to manipulate the minds and exploit the Islamic faith for their own political and personal gains...

All leading to the exploitation of vast amounts of American Tax Dollars via the military mafia's or Beltway Bandits getting their hands on Big Government Defence spending under Reagan and Bush policies.

I think the American Forefathers did not conceive that Article 1 Section 8 of The Constitution of the United States of America would be used for such corrupt personal agendas...

This is a short synopsis of what was going on during the Iran-Contra and Iraqgate under Reagan/Bush. The supporting of both Iran and Iraq as they killed each other off for American Defence profits.

Policies that ultimately undermined the U.S. National Security interest, and allowed "Beltway Bandits" to gain vast resources and power to control and shape the Bush(s) political and Defence policies of the United States that cost America Trillions of Dollars, and adversely affected the World economy in the future.

The 1980 official connections between the Mujahedeen and their "Radicalization of Islam" and the connection with U.S.A. Central Intelligence Agency (CIA). This is also a great place to note the connections of the Saudi Royal Family and their extended family member Osama Bin Ladin who rises to power via the funding and partnerships of the U.S. and Saudi "Wahhabism" or "Radical Islam."

This was the days of Jimmy Carter and the rise of the Republican Intelligence community, i.e. the CIA and the H. W. Bush who would later become Vice President and then President supported by the illicit funds from this agenda...

The front man became Ronald Reagan as Bush came out of the shadows of the CIA... As you can see America became the number one exporter of the Weapons of War and the game of "War and Rumours of War"...

It was the misguided Reagan and Bush(s) policies that later came back to haunt American National Security on 9/11... Saudi did not give anything for nothing. Saudi gained vast military base build up, real estate holdings near those bases, contracts for the development and the brokering of weapons. All paid for by American Tax Dollars under the Reagan/Bush Big Government Defence Spending policies...

Overcoming policy making obstacles is difficult, especially, where there are drug related involvements...

The first obstacle is the lure of money and the allegations that drug sales apparently has always been part of the covert agendas

The second obstacle is the long standing realities that drugs have been a part of covert policy. One of many examples is Heroin from Vietnam, Southeast Asia that became known as the "French Connection"…

Guns, Drugs and Jihad inception and money laundering primary area starts here in the Khyber Pass in the North West section of Pakistan bordering Afghanistan where most of the drugs/heroin is funnelled through…

BCCI and other groups launder billions of dollars through the U.S./ISI Narcotics operations…

The Saudi Royal Family also buys into this network of illicit drug trade.

The funds that are later used for the purchase of a variety of Saudi Royal Family assets via the Bin Ladin connections.

These drug connections not only come from Bin Ladin, but other Saudi Royal Family Members. They expand into other drugs such as Cocaine that is shipped from U.S./Saudi Intelligence connections in Latin American and into the U.S. market and French Market where a Saudi Prince got arrested.

I feel that many of those assets also included Disney Stocks in France and the U.S…

We really need to establish some guidelines for covert CIA and/or DEA Drug Operations that related to the distribution of drugs… Then we need to know what resources can be allocated for such policies…

Robert Gates has had a long-standing relationship with Crooks and Criminals so he should know... Allegations claim that he climbed from Capo to CIA Director to Defence Secretary.

He continued and enhanced the guns, drugs and Jihad agenda and has participated in Trillions of Tax Dollars being divvied out to this old and strongly established network under Regan, Bush(s) and even entrenched so strongly that President Obama kept him as Secretary of Defence...

6
ATTENTION CONSTRUCTIVE POLICY MAKERS

I'm not just talking to America's; I'm talking to the entire World... You will come to learn from my "THE UNELECTED PRESIDENT" book series that I have dealt with major political policy issues around the world and I have come to learn that humanity must make personal changes or perish...

We must solve problems in a more civil society way. Our drug of choice should be education and the betterment of Civil Society. If we can do this there will be far more opportunities for everyone...

Military Strategy is complex. For over 20 years, I have wondered if the end justified the means. Did the invasion suppress the lucrative drug traffic or just promote it? On the other hand, perhaps it only put the business into more powerful and ruthless hand...

Then there is the covet Government involvement from rogue elements... I certainly wasn't happy to see unclassified documents of the Iran-Contra affair. CIA Director Bush before he became President had did gun running trades with General Noriega of Panama, and that several DEA agents got their hands caught in the cookie jar dealing with Noriega also...

These days Drugs due to the major downturn in economic policy blunders of the previous Administrations tend to go together.. Economic hardships is one of the main reasons why so many states are discussing legalizing the growing and distribution of marijuana...

Since 9/11 drug consumption and use has went up many fold... The problem is a huge threat to America's economic/national security... Military intervention has little affect and the long haul process of obtaining an education and lifting one above drugs and social oppression is often shelved in favor of the short run buck in hand...

"Diplomatic suggestions" do not always turn out well... The Devil has a tendency to get into the details... My suggestions in Panama was muted by a lack of economic focus that created a much larger demand...

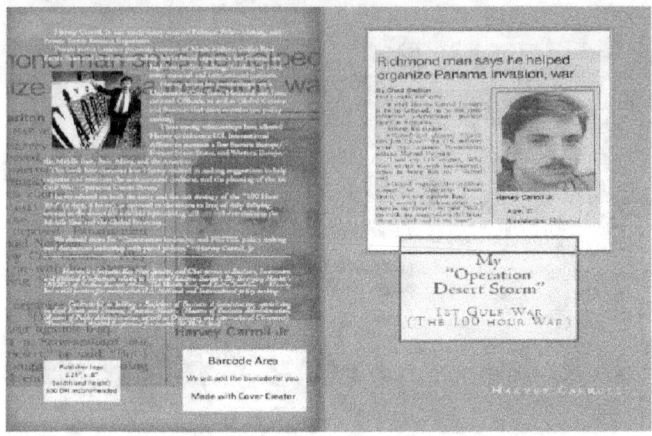

My work on both "Operation Just Cause" and "Desert Storm" 1st Gulf War was success, but built profiteers that influenced political policy to return to the Gulf. If you read my books on the 1st Gulf War you will find out that which undermined Americas economic and national security…

In Somalia, a simple "Missionary Mission" got that turned into a Military Mission that resulted in "Black Hawk Down"; very silly how trying to feed people was turned into a conflict...

My advice is to be careful, and try to make sure that "Diplomacy" or any constructive military actions are followed to the letter…

Try to have a primary focus on constructive ways of establishing policy. Sound policy creation can create solid long-term relations, which will add economic values...

A focus on constructive policy making with "Economic Visions and Values" give people a much stronger feeling of hope to cling to. As apposed to going for the quick buck, and selling their soul to the Devil that devours ones hopes, ambitions and talents.

This is why I think this policy suggestion in dealing with the Mexican, border issue is much more constructive and proactive in dealing with cross border immigration and drug cartel issues.

7
BUILD A WALL
OR
BUILD SOCIETY

Is there a problem with Drugs and Illegal Immigration from the Mexican Border? YES;

However, Diplomatic Relations between the United States and Mexico can turn these economic, and immigration issues into something constructive for both countries. If we try... But will that be in the form of building a Trump Wall, a Solar Power Wall, Housing Condo Wall, or more focus on "Comprehensive Planning" and my M-AID plan... Or a hybrid of all...

So, how can we provide jobs, opportunities that benefit America, keep immigrants out of the welfare system and out of jail, and improve worker skills, and bridge language issues? My solution is M-AID FUND.

My M-AID FUND could be a U.S./Mexico Joint Venture and a UN Development Project. A worldwide capital market funds syndicated to develop vast growth projects.

M-AID FUND could increase Mexican labor opportunities. It should be designed to provide economic development and investment growth opportunities to increase jobs for both Mexico and America...

Large scale projects such as building ring and railroads around key cities. A simple no brainer that spurs growth and economic development... Perhaps build new Cities in joint venture near the border like "The Venus Project" http://www.youtube.com/watch?v=gJ fKXbvA5T8&feature=fvwrel and this more lengthy part

New ring and rail projects provide

many new sites for land development of office, logistics/industrial, apartments, housing communities as well as retail shops.

I feel that we could develop a mass organized migrant worker/labor camp concept where thousands of Mexicans are allowed to enter the U.S. stay in "Mexican, American Infrastructure Development Funded United Nations Directorate (M-AID FUND) camps.

M-AID Camps that will help America develop infrastructure projects much like large scale Military/Corps of Engineer projects or the TVA post-Depression days.

While in the Army, I used to participate in mass mobilization of tens of thousands of troops, and the rail heading of hundreds of tanks across Germany in just a few short hours...

Once there the mission went into

effect. Some times that involved establishing temporary housing, and the building of roads, airfields, and so forth...

So, it is reasonable to use the same concept to successful develop mass infrastructure projects throughout America in and around key cities...

Here is the basic concept of more developed housing as the plan progresses. Rail Road housing; not the WWII Cattle Cars filled with slave labor, but decent mobile housing that can be railed into areas and set up on rail spurs.

This mobile housing can establish jobs for migrant workers. Such mobile labor movement can add real value by developing American infrastructure projects to spurs growth and development.

These mobile work camps would

supply reasonable wages in safe and secure surroundings and provide respect and pride in U.S./Mexico relations instead of disputes over border issues.

Before, people start thinking this is silly. I remind you that the American Military and the U.N. has built mobile cities in Iraq and Afghanistan using Military forces, and contract labor to build infrastructure in those areas today...

So, why would it not work in America as well? All while increasing America`s GDP, providing new Tax Base Jobs for Immigrant Workers and Americans alike and creating investment opportunities for World Wide Capital Markets...

I dubbed this concept the "Ring Road and Rail Revolution" which is a thought that I have been pushing for quite some time. A revolution of ideas that focus on spurring large-scale economic development projects throughout America and solving the border dispute issue.

This thought come to me a while back; however, the M-AID FUND came to me on Christmas Eve 2009; the birthday eve of a great carpenter and builder of some 2000 years ago.

I have been inspired to change the way we view of drugs and immigration from Latin America/Mexico is viewed, and the way our Defense and Diplomacy funds are to be used in the future. I call for those funds to be used in a more constructive, peaceful and prosperous way...

About the Author
"THE UNELECTED PRESIDENT"

"Operation Just Cause"
My suggestion for the
United States invasion of Panama
By
Harvey Carroll, Jr.

I'm a former U.S. Army Military Policeman/Investigator, whom has seen shocking drug related deaths, and investigators bloody shot-out brains laying on their car seats... This view led me to believe in the need for a real "War on Drugs" the result "Operation Just Cause" the Invasion of Panama...

I now hold a Bachelors of Business Administration Degree specializing in Real Estate and Finance, and three partial Masters in Business, Public Administration as well as Diplomacy and International Commerce...

I've been considered the most influential international political figure in Kentucky-US, and some would say that perhaps in the World at one time. I have dealt with Governors, Senators, Presidents and Foreign Heads of State; and in the process I have saved millions of lives, and affected the economic fate of nations... Yet, I have made mistakes, and even cost lives and often ponder if the "End Justified the Means."

It has always been quite easy for me to deal with complex U.S. National and International Policy. From a young age I dealt with local, state, national and international policy that includes Latin America i.e. "Panama," Middle East (Iraq, Libya, Syria, Israel, Iran), Africa, and even coming to the AID after the collapse of the Soviet Union to protect U.S. and Global Security by suggesting buying out the nuclear weapons to prevent them from ending up on the Black Market for Terrorism, as well as preventing the former fifteen Soviet States against each other.

I also suggested financial bailouts, and another financial AID via the IFC/World Bank for Ukraine that saved seventy-five banks a few years ago (a similar plan presented to the U.S. House and Senate Financial Services Committee "Frank and Dodd" to bailout the American Economy to assist 2/3rds of the American States and Top Banks from Collapse.

More recently, I have shared suggestions to have the OSCE get between the separatist and the Ukrainian Army to the Ukrainian Presidents people tasked to negotiate the Minsk Agreements that may have prevented Ukraine from turning into another Syria... In the process I have noticed that Russian President Putin sent Troops "Little Green Men" into Crimea much like my suggestions for the "Panama Invasion,.." which you're about to read...